Good Rhymes, Good Times

Original poems by Lee Bennett Hopkins

Illustrated by Frané Lessac

HarperCollins*Publishers*

To Charles John Egita
For city and country
good times!
—L. B. H.

For Philip
—F. L.

GOOD RHYMES, GOOD TIMES
Text copyright © 1995 by Lee Bennett Hopkins
Illustrations copyright © 1995 by Frané Lessac
Printed in the U.S.A. All rights reserved.

Library of Congress Cataloging-in-Publication Data
Hopkins, Lee Bennett.
    Good rhymes, good times : original poems / by Lee Bennett
Hopkins ; illustrated by Frané Lessac.
        p.   cm.
    Summary: A collection of original poems ranging in topic from
sounds in the city to the seasons to bedtime.
        ISBN 0-06-023499-7. — ISBN 0-06-023500-4 (lib. bdg.)
        I. Children's poetry, American.   [I. American poetry.]
I. Lessac, Frané, ill.   II. Title.
PS3558.O63544P64   1995   93-8159
811'.54—dc20   CIP
                                                      AC

Typography by Elynn Cohen
    1 2 3 4 5 6 7 8 9 10
                ❖
            First Edition

~ Contents ~

Sing a Song of Cities	5
Behind the Museum Door	6
Mother's Plea	8
Puppy	9
Overnight at the Vet's	10
Cat's Kit	11
Valentine Feelings	12
Kite	14
Split	17
No Matter	18
Autumn's Beginning	19
Treasure	20
This Tooth	21
Winner	22
Donna	23
The Day After Christmas	24
Snow City	26
Winter	27
Good Books, Good Times!	28
Bedtime	30
Nighttime	31

~ Sing a Song of Cities ~

Sing a song of cities.
If you do,
Cities will sing back to you.

They'll sing in subway roars and rumbles.
People-laughs, machine-loud-grumbles.

Sing a song of cities.
If you do,
Cities will sing back to you.

~ Behind the Museum Door ~

What's behind the museum door?

Ancient necklaces,
African art,
Armor of knights,
A peasant cart;

Pioneer wagons,
Vintage cars,
A planetarium

ceilinged

with stars;

Priceless old coins,
A king's golden throne,
Mummies in linen,

And

A dinosaur bone.

~ Mother's Plea ~

Silence sirens.

Hush all horns.

Quiet rumbling
    traffic
    roars.

Please,
City,
    have
    some
    pity.

Promise me
    not
    one
    more
    beep?

My newborn
    pigeons
    need
    their
    sleep.

~ Puppy ~

We bought our puppy
    A brand new bed
But he likes sleeping
    On mine instead.

I'm glad he does
    'Cause I'd miss his cold nose

Waking me up,
    Tickling my toes.

~ Overnight at the Vet's ~

I found
a strand
of snow-white hair

strewn upon his
favorite chair.

I wonder how
he's feeling there

alone—

I wonder
if he wants
his bone.

I wonder
if he'll catch
a flea—

I wonder
if
he
misses
me.

~ Cat's Kit ~

Needle-claws
Thimbled paws

Soft,
　　silky,
　　　　pincushiony toes—

A
Siamese
seamstress

wherever

she
goes.

~ Valentine Feelings ~

I feel

    flippy,
    fizzy,
    whoopy,
    whizzy.

I'm feeling wonderful.
I'm feeling just fine.

Because

    YOU

gave

    ME

A valentine.

~ Kite ~

The new kite
blue-white,

flitters
twirls
tumbles
twitters

like
a
young bird

in

the
wide-awake
sky.

~ Split ~

Flash.
   Roar.
      More.

Keep it coming.

C'mon,
Soar.

It's *your* night
to fight
for flight.

Go wander.
Go wonder.

Go!

Go split
the sky
wondrous
thunder.

~ No Matter ~

No matter
how
hot-burning
it
is
outside

when

you peel
a
long, fat cucumber

or

cut deep
into
a
fresh, ripe watermelon

coolness

comes
into
your
hands.

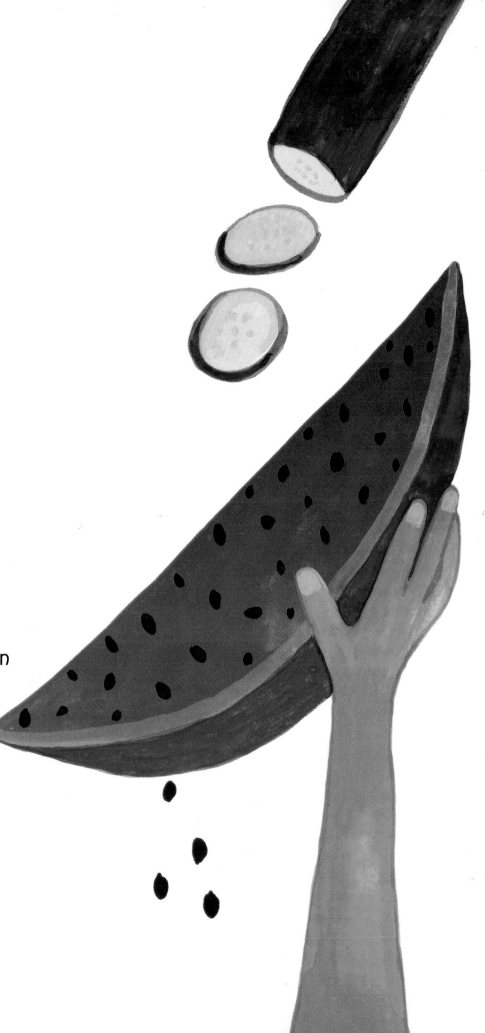

~ Autumn's Beginning ~

A
monarch butterfly
quietly
perched
itself
upon
a
pumpkin.

Orange
on
orange

Autumn
came

officially

that
very
moment.

~ Treasure ~

A rusty door key,
A part of a tool,
A dead bee I was saving
        to take in to school;

A crust of pizza,
Sand from the shore,
A piece of lead pipe,
An old apple core;

My library card,
A small model rocket—

I guess
it
is
time

to
clean
out
my
pocket.

~ This Tooth ~

I jiggled it
    jaggled it
    jerked it.

I pushed
    and pulled
    and poked it.

But—

As soon as I stopped,
and left it alone,
This tooth came out
on its very own!

~ Winner ~

Burst out
Brussels sprout.

You're going
to be
a winner.

A million-dollar
jackpot
for a cold
December
dinner.

~ Donna ~

She
likes
getting
toys

that
make
lots
of
noise

especially
the
kind
that
will

SCARE

all
the
boys.

~ The Day After Christmas ~

Trash cans
wrapped
with
torn papers
from
my
presents

wear

a
bow
of
snow.

~ Snow City ~

The snow glides quietly

       d

        o

         w

          n

Filling the air
      with a magical hush

But tomorrow the snow
      will make everyone frown
For the streets will be filled
      with a magical

             M U S H !

~ Winter ~

NEVER

quarrel

with
winter.

It

ALWAYS

wins.

~ Good Books, Good Times! ~

Good books.
Good times.
Good stories.
Good rhymes.
Good beginnings.
Good ends.
Good people.
Good friends.
Good fiction.
Good facts.
Good adventures.
Good acts.
Good stories.
Good rhymes.
Good books.
Good times.

~ Bedtime ~

Can I have a glass of water?
Can I sip some apple juice?
Can I say good night to Daddy?
Will you read me Dr. Seuss?

Will I see you in the morning?
Won't you please keep on the light?

Oh—

If only I could find a way
To chase
       away
            the
                night.

~ Nighttime ~

How do dreams know
        when to creep

Into my head
        when I fall off
        to sleep?